Wick's
Punctuation Rules
for Court Reporters

Workbook

Kenneth A. Wick

Wick's Punctuation Rules
for Court Reporters:
Workbook
(October 2023)

Table of Contents

Introduction

This book contains 600 punctuation and formatting exercises for *Wick's Punctuation Rules for Court Reports.*

Because it is not possible for a student to master punctuation and formatting by simply reading a textbook, practice is necessary. The student's goal should be to learn the punctuation and formatting rules in the textbook and then practice the rules in the workbook. This way the rules become ingrained.

The workbook exercises are arranged to follow the rule order as presented in *Wick's Punctuation Rules for Court Reports.* There are 475 exercises that are punctuation or formatting specific (comma, semicolon, number formatting, and so on) and focus on one or more textbook rules. There are 125 "general" exercises that randomly cover the textbook punctuation and formatting rules.

Note: *Wick's Punctuation Rules for Court Reports: Workbook* is an expansion (100 additional exercises) and revision of *The Essential 99 Punctuation Rules for Court Reporters: Workbook.*

This page is blank.

Essential Grammar

Identifying an Independent or Dependent Clause
Exercises for Rules G3 to G6.

Place parentheses, ( ), around an independent clause and brackets, [ ], around a dependent clause.

1. Everyone was busy, and I went to the movie alone.
2. I will see if the book has arrived.
3. Mary needs to check back tomorrow before the store opens.
4. I'm counting calories, but I really want dessert.
5. Cats are good pets because they are clean.
6. Tommy dragged a chair across the wood floor while his mother watched in horror.
7. Tommy, who is 11 years old, was scolded by his mother.
8. The mistake that you made will be corrected.
9. I don't know where the keys are.
10. Her mom was pleased when she got the job.
11. As you read the textbook, you will find the answers that you are looking for.
12. He ran out of money, yet he didn't stop playing poker.
13. I drove to school with a friend.
14. I dove my car that recently got new brakes.
15. I do not know how far it is to school.
16. Mary lives one floor above you.
17. Our secretary, who is never late, called in sick at 9:00 a.m.
18. I do not know who gave you the flu.
19. The client said that he would call us next week.
20. When he calls, tell him our rates have slightly increased.

Identifying a Coordinating Conjunction, Conjunctive Adverb, Transitional Expression, or Parenthetical Expression
Exercises for Rules G7 to G9.

Place parentheses, ( ), around a coordinating conjunction and brackets, [ ], around a conjunctive adverb, transitional expression, or parenthetical expression.

21. Everyone was busy, and I went to the movie alone.
22. Sally didn't want to go to the dentist; therefore, she canceled.
23. He ran out of money, yet he didn't stop playing poker.
24. I lost my job. Consequently, my car was repossessed.
25. I left 30 minutes early; however, an accident still made me late.
26. To tell you the truth, I hate Monday mornings.
27. I saw the suspect. In fact, I can recall what he was wearing.

Identifying a Prepositional or Verbal Phrase
Exercises for Rules G10 and G11.

Place parentheses, ( ), around a prepositional phrase and brackets, [ ], around a verbal phrase.

28. Don't step on the broken glass.
29. Seeing his excellent test score, he fainted.
30. The dog jump in the car.
31. The book on the table is now missing.
32. To provide a safe work environment, security cameras were installed.
33. Robert lives in the apartment around the corner.
34. Strong-minded to get the cookies on top of the refrigerator, Tommy dragged a chair across the floor.

Determining an Essential or Nonessential Element
Exercises for Rules G12 and G13.

Place parentheses, ( ), around an essential element and brackets, [ ], around a nonessential element. Insert commas if necessary.

35. A man who wore black is the suspect.
36. Brandon who wore black is the suspect.
37. The officer arrived in a black and white car a patrol car.
38. The Defendant Mr. Smith hired a private attorney.
39. A psychologist Dr. Cooper is highly respected.
40. Amber's psychologist Dr. Cooper is highly respected.

4

The Period

Exercises for Rules 1 to 5.

Properly place the period. Capitalize the following word if necessary (Rule 138).

41. I passed the test
42. I passed the test we went out to dinner
43. Please speak up
44. Can you state and spell your full name for the record
45. I object the question is beyond the scope
46. Objection the question is vague
47. Objection ambiguous compound
48. Hurry we're going to be late
49. Crap I don't know
50. All right fine we can take a recess now

The Comma

Introductory Clause or Phrase
Exercises for Rules 6 to 8.

Properly place the comma.

51. To provide a safe work environment security cameras were installed.
52. On reaching Nevada we stopped at the first place we could gamble.
53. Running out of money he didn't stop playing poker.
54. On the concrete sidewalk our dog sat obediently.
55. To tell you the truth I hate Monday mornings.
56. Across the street a squirrel darted with a nut.
57. Because they are clean cats are good pets.
58. In 2018 91 people graduated from the small elementary school.
59. He said he was not in town yesterday. However many people saw him.
60. While his mother watched in horror Tommy dragged a chair across the wood floor.

Compound or Complex Sentence
Exercises for Rules 9 to 12.

Properly place the comma.

61. I lost my job last week and my car was repossessed.
62. I'm counting calories but I really want dessert.
63. Linda was telling the truth or she was telling a huge lie.
64. Everyone was busy so I went to the movie alone.
65. He ran out of money yet he didn't stop playing poker.
66. The dentist but he went anyway.
67. I worked ten days last month yet able to pay the rent.
68. You should tell the whole story or face the consequences.
69. He said he was not in town yesterday but recognizing his obvious lie he made up a cover story.
70. Tammy could not decide what to do and to tell you the truth she had to slept on it.

Series of Items
Exercises for Rules 13 to 16.

Properly place the comma.

71. I need to buy milk and bread.
72. I need to buy milk eggs and bread.
73. I need to buy milk eggs bread.
74. I need to buy milk and eggs and bread.
75. Please invite John Sue Liam and Sarah to the meeting
76. A court reporting student needs a steno machine a computer the textbooks et cetera.
77. A court reporting student needs to buy the textbook the workbook a notebook et cetera before the first day of instruction.
78. Did you mail the invitations and response cards and directions to the guests?
79. Did you mail the invitations response cards and directions to the guests?
80. Did you mail the case file to Mr. Smith at Clark Garcia Jones & Smith?

Nonessential Element, Interrupting Element, or Participle Phrase.
Exercises for Rules 17 to 20.

Properly place the comma.

81. He said that he was not in town yesterday. Many people however saw him.
82. Mary Sue who is my half sister was born in 1994.
83. I upon arriving at the accident scene fainted at the sight of blood.
84. It happened you know right after like dinner.
85. The original document was important containing the first photograph of the accident scene
86. The motion filed just yesterday with the Court was immediately denied by the judge.
87. I don't' like the looks of this to tell you the truth.
88. My situation in so many words is bad.
89. NewLeaf Recycling which started in this city 15 years ago is relocating to Chicago.
90. Janet shouted the answer bursting with confidence.

Contrasting Phrase, Direct Address, or Coordinate Adjective
Exercises for Rules 21 to 23.

Properly place the comma.

91. I briskly walk never jog one hour each day.
92. I said Mr. Ogawa not Mrs. Ogawa.
93. It will be another hot windy day.
94. His cruel callous actions demanded a severe sentence.
95. The old ghost town is not on the map.
96. The smart charismatic employee quickly promoted to shift manager.
97. Please approach the bench Ms. Anderson.
98. Explain what you mean sir by "gently used"?
99. The attorneys conferred off the record not on the record.
100. Please speak up ma'am.

Title or Degree with a Personal Name;
Jr. or Sr.; an Appositive; or an Enumeration
Exercises for Rules 24 to 27.

Properly place the comma.

101. Did Dr. Smith your primary care physician see you last week?
102. The tree tall and strong withstood the strong winds.
103. Dr. Jones of South Carolina Family Healthcare Group is my physical therapist.
104. Did you invite Melody Jones Esq. to the briefing?
105. Katy Banks PhD is schedule to testify on Tuesday.
106. Ron Davies Jr. is also attending the briefing.
107. Did you hear Mr. Jones III died last week?
108. Did you know William Jones Sr. founded the law firm?
109. What gifts do I want? First a gift certificate to Ulta. Beauty. Second dinner at my favorite restaurant.
110. Make sure to include the following on your application: one a contact email; two the best time to call you; and three a contact email.

Yes and No
Exercises for Rule 28.

Properly write the comma or period with *yes* and *no*. Capitalize if necessary (Rule 138).

Do you work for the San Jose Police Department?
111. Yes I do.
112. I do not no.
113. I work for the County of Santa Clara no.

Did you see Jenny leave the office that day?
114. Yes she left with James around 4:30 p.m.
115. I worked until 5:00 p.m. that day no.
116. No I did not see her leave.

Where you speeding at the time of the accident?
117. No I was not speeding.
118. No I was driving about 35 miles per hour.
119. The posted speed limit is 35 no.
120. I was not no.

**The Words *Please, Too, Including, Such As,* or *Like*;
or *Inc.* or *LLC* in a Business Name**
Exercises for Rules 29 to 34.

Properly place the comma.

121. Darn I spilled coffee on my pants.
122. Now let's move on to the next problem.
123. Will you please turnoff your cell phone.
124. Will you turnoff your cell phone please.
125. He's not just an actor; he's a singer too.
126. She too enjoys swimming
127. The zoo has a variety of animals such as lions and elephants.
128. We visited famous landmarks including the Eiffel Tower and the Colosseum.
129. Tech Solutions Inc. organized the conference.
130. Tech Solutions Inc.—for the first time since the pandemic—organized the conference.

The Semicolon

Compound Sentences
Exercises for Rules 39 to 42.

Properly place the semicolon and any associated comma. For additional practice, use a period were acceptable.

131. Richard does not like broccoli he hates it.
132. My father's ancestors are from Germany my mother's ancestors are from England.
133. I saw James in the corner of my eye unfortunately I did not see which direction he went.
134. I did my homework however I did the wrong set of problems.
135. Ashley was the only person who could make the decision therefore she weighed the evidence carefully.
136. She weighed the evidence as a result the decision was sound.
137. I told the truth as I see it - I told the whole truth.
138. I like him to be honest - I love him.
139. I saw the accident my husband saw nothing.

140. I saw James in the corner of my eye thus I did not see which direction he went.
141. I bought a new 15-inch laptop, cell phone, and tablet and I planned to set them up over the holiday weekend.
142. As I entered the room, I noticed the lights flickering and if I had not left immediately, I would be in the dark
143. Jack loves Melissa in fact he sent her flowers.
144. Jack sent Melissa flowers hence he loves her.
145. Jack sent Melissa flowers however he forgot the card.

Series of Items
Exercises for Rules 43 and 44.

Properly place semicolons or replace commas with semicolons.

146. The Defendant has lived in New York City, New York, San Francisco, California, and Detroit, Michigan.
147. Please grab the red ring of keys, the car keys, a bottle of water from the refrigerator, and my lunch.
148. I arrived at work at 9:30 a.m., turned on my computer, and called Denise, the director's secretary.
149. The officer stated that he contacted the people living at the address of the complaint given five minutes earlier by dispatch that he talked to the people living at the address about the recent noise complaint of the party and that he advised the people living at the address to turn down the volume on the large stereo system.
150. My next available times are Wednesday, 9:00 a.m., Thursday, 1:30 p.m., and Friday, 10:30 a.m.
151. The account payments were received on June 9, 2022, July 11, 2022, August 6, 2022, and September 10, 2022.
152. I consulted with my lawyer, Ms. Anderson, my CPA, Mr. Smith, and an expert in the field, Ms. Cooper.
153. I invited Jim, the office manager, Joan, the financial manager, and Linda, the supervisor.

The Words *For Example, Namely,* or *That is*
Exercises for Rule 45.

Properly place all punctuation.

154. The software comes with several useful features for example data encryption.

155. The exhibit features various types of art namely paintings, sculptures, and photograph.
156. The project requires specific skills that is data analysis and project management are essential.
157. The instructions are straightforward who to contact in an emergency namely the manager.
158. The recipe calls for a few essential ingredients namely flour, sugar, and eggs.

Enumerated Phrases
Exercises for Rule 46.

Properly place all punctuation.

159. The reasons for the employment termination were 1 excessive tardiness 2 substandard work quality and 3 arguing with other employees.
160. I quit my last job because A the manager was verbally abusive B better pay and C better benefits.

The Colon
Exercises for Rules 47 to 51.

Properly place the colon. Capitalize if necessary.

161. Luke did not know the new law all bicyclists must wear helmets.
162. Amy is afraid of only one bug spiders.
163. He had his favorite meal that evening soup, steak, and French fries.
164. The accident report contained one glaring fact he was traveling well above the speed limit based on the skid marks.
165. The following law enforcement agencies were at the scene of the accident a sheriff, an NYPD officer, and a detective.
166. An attorney advised me about my claim there was probably not enough evidence to win in court.
167. THE COURT Juror No. 5 is dismissed.
168. Susan passed the skills test her endless hours of practice paid off.

169. These are the reasons for the increase in Bay Area home sales economic recovery and low-interest rates.
170. I want you to understand that I saw a large, hairy thing that night a Bigfoot.
171. The sign at the construction site states, "Caution Hard Hat Area."
172. MS. ANDERSON The witness has not been qualified as an expert.
173. John failed to make the job candidate list he was just shy of the experience requirement.
174. She had two things on her mind rushing to get ready for work turn off the iron and remember the case file.
175. We know the reason for the murder money.

The Dash
Exercises for Rules 52 to 62.

Properly place the Dash.

176. I took borrowed the money.
177. I'll be frank with you mark my words because this is the honest truth I did not steal the money.
178. Q Did you steal
    A No.
    Q the money?
179. Q How long did it take you to recover
    A Four months.
    Q from the surgery?
180. The primary defense team Tom, Sue, and I was retained on April 2, 2022.
181. The needed food bread, milk, and cheese was bought on the way home.
182. Tom, Sue, and I the primary defense team was retained on April 2, 2022.
183. The need food strike that. Did you stop on the way home?
184. Q Were you speeding
    A I need a break.
    Q After this question. at the time of the accident?
185. Did you buy correction stop on the way home.

The Question Mark

Exercises for Rules 63 to 72.

Properly place the appropriate missing punctuation. Capitalize if necessary.

186. She's right isn't she?
187. He proposed to you Saturday evening correct?
188. There were two suspects wasn't there in the vehicle?
189. The children were excited were they not that Christmas morning?
190. You were headed southbound is that not correct during the evening commute?
191. Were two suspects in the vehicle I'm talking about after you witnessed the robbery.
192. You were headed southbound is that a good statement?
193. The defendant wore a blue jacket do you remember?
194. You were headed southbound isn't that correct?
195. She drove didn't she southbound?
196. You have never lived in a big city have you?
197. I'm right am I not that you've only lived out in the country?
198. You have only lived out in the country right?
199. What I asked was did you date the Plaintiff in 2021?
200. The question is simply this where were you that day?
201. You were headed southbound do you remember?
202. Was his coat red white blue?
203. Did you ever think how is my father doing after his hip replacement?
204. What were you doing before the accident. Using the cell phone.
205. My last question was you saw Dr. Cooper on January 11, 2018?

The Quotation Mark

Punctuation Marks
Exercises for Rules 78 to 80.

Correct, if necessary, the period, comma, semicolon, or colon.

206. Freddie screamed, "fire".
207. "Let's go out for dinner", Rory said.

208. Linda turned the TV to a "nature show:" a shark feeding frenzy.
209. Tom said, "grab one;" "grab what", Mindy responded.
210. Susan asked "Are you feeling lucky today"?
211. "I'm flying to Detroit", Tom signed. "You go where the work is".

Direct Quotations
Exercises for Rules 73 to 76.

Properly place the quotation marks and other missing punctuation. Capitalize if necessary.

212. The officer said drop it.
213. She replied I'm going to quit this job if I don't get a raise.
214. James said I'll drop it off on my way home.
215. Put your hands on your head the officer instructed.
216. I got the job I squealed
217. The police report states at 3:17 p.m., a stolen-car call was received.
218. The code section stipulates all persons shall give a notice of 30 days.
219. Don't hit your brother Tammy said sternly. You must learn to share.
220. I'm going to quit this job she replied if I don't get a raise.
221. Rachel asked what do you want for dinner tonight?
222. Did Rachel ask what do you want for dinner tonight?
223. Did Angela say I'm making spaghetti for dinner?
224. The officer said quote drop it unquote.
225. William replied quote/unquote I quit.
226. The code section states quote all persons shall give a notice of 30 days.
227. The report stated the important detail on page 3 at 3:17 p.m., a stolen-car call was received.
228. The officer was forceful in his instructions drop it.
229. Peter said I don't understand the detailed instructions.
230. Amy responded I know the laws in this state.
231. I could not tell you Tim responded what Andrew's problem is.
232. The tax on the car is over $3,000 Randy gasped.
233. I think the suspect said quote give me your wallet close quote.

234. Did the suspect say quote/unquote give me your wallet?
235. Deborah asked how much did it cost to fix the car?

Titles, Special Emphasis, or *So-Called*
Exercises for Rules 81 to 83.

Properly place the quotation marks.

236. The document is titled Know Your Punctuation.
237. Ann's favorite *Home and Garden TV* show episode is Backyard Décor.
238. Due to Jack's previous jail escape, he is labeled high risk.
239. Mr. Wright said he bought a chopper, a gun, while on parole.
240. The so-called experts failed to predict the current economic situation.
241. Have you seen the *Star Trek* episode The Enemy Within?
242. What did the Defendant, Mr. Smith, mean by self-help?
243. To answer your question, I recommend reading The New You chapter in the bestseller *Be Your Best*.
244. Success involves hard work; there is no so-called easy route.

Mispronounced or Made-Up Word;
Definition or Translation
Exercises for Rules 84 to 87.

Properly place the appropriate punctuation.

245. The hilarious joke made me snickernoodle with laughter.
      Note: Snickernoodle is a made-up word.
246. Amy went NUCLEAR with the comment.
      Note: *Nuclear* pronounced Nuk-ler.
247. I met with Charles SHERBET on October 14.
      Note: *Sherbet* pronounced Sher-bert, not Sher-bit.
248. The dictionary defines *zeitgeist* as the general intellectual, moral, and cultural climate of an era.
249. Did Peter Yogi Berra play for the New York Yankees?

15

The Apostrophe

Singular and Plural Word Possessive
Exercises for Rules 88 to 91.

Properly write or correct the apostrophe in each sentence.

250. Someone stole the plaintiffs purse from the courtroom.
251. Have you seen Aprils missing wallet?
252. Childrens toys are so expensive.
253. My brother-in-laws testimony did not help the case.
254. I want to hear the next two witnesses testimony.
255. I need to get my BOSS-EZ approval. [Spoken: Boss-ez]
256. The professors research is groundbreaking.

Various Possessive Rules
Exercises for Rules 92 to 98.

Properly write or correct the apostrophe in each sentence.

257. Tom claimed the heavy lifting violated workers rights.
258. I bought some fresh produce at the farmers market.
259. The months gas bill is higher than last months.
260. The Presidents speechs main message was unity.
261. The homework of my daughters friend was found stuffed in the backpacks pocket.
262. The storm undid a weeks worth of yard work.
263. How do you think the girls soccer team will do this year?
264. Dont use the boys restroom by mistake.
265. I gave my two weeks notice at work.

Plural of a Letter or Misread Word; Omission of a Letter or Figure; Certain Verb Forms
Exercises for Rules 99 to 103.

Properly write or correct the apostrophe in each sentence.

266. Is there one or two Ls in traveled?
267. Each judge has their dos and donts
    Note: *dos and donts* used as plural of do and don't.
268. I spell my name, Bret, with one t, not two ts.
269. I sold my 68 Ford Mustang.

270. Hana doesn't recall. Her surgery was in either 2017 or 18.
271. Did you say *talkin* or *walkin*?
272. Cindy x-ed out the spelling mistake and wrote the correction above.
273. Patrick IDd the suspect handcuffed in the patrol car.
274. I 86d the junk straight into the trashcan.

The Hyphen

Prefix and Suffix
Exercises for Rules 104 to 107.

Properly use the hyphen in each sentence.

275. Who won the county wide race in District 2?
276. Were there any post operative complications?
277. The illegal firearms found in the raid consisted mostly of semi-automatic rifles.
278. The witness corrected his statement and remarked the exhibit.
279. I invest in both long and short-term securities.
280. On Tuesdays, the board has both an open and closed-door session.
281. I lived on a small coop until 14 years old.
282. Do you have and preThanksgiving traditions?
283. Focus groups were divided into 20, 30, and 40-year-olds.
284. As I recall, I had a hotel room on the twenty-second or third floor.
285. The fashion was retro: 1970 like.

Compound and Spelled-Out Words
Exercises for Rules 108 to 116.

Properly use compound words and/or the hyphen in each sentence.

286. I once saw a group of zookeepers capture a man eating alligator.
287. Are there any cross references for the compound adjective rules in *The Chicago Manual of Style*?

288. Please check the time table to see what time the bus arrives.
289. I was short changed by the cashier.
290. Did you have your suit dry cleaned before the start of the trial?
291. A high level meeting was scheduled after the annual budget was not approved.
292. I feared a worst case situation: layoffs.
293. However, the bottom line results were no raises or overtime.
294. This caused a year of penny pinching purchases and decisions.
295. I hope the budget crisis is not a long lasting problem.
296. The are you seriously that freaking stupid look stopped me cold.
297. The fast paced and lopsided football game ended in our favor.
298. The newly formed football team needed more practice.
299. I received a how are you doing after all these years? welcome.
300. The old coal mining town is a popular hiking destination.
301. The house used A frame architecture.
302. Is your position at the law firm fulltime or parttime?
303. The x ray technician x rayed my arm in four different angles or positions.
304. My last name is Schmidt, S c h m i d t, not Smith.
305. My name is Staci Green, S t a c i G r, double, e n.

The Ellipsis and Slash
Exercises for Rules 117 to 119.

Properly use the slash or ellipsis in each sentence.

Direct quotation for practice problems:

> "The factory fire on September 14, 2022, was caused by human error. In this case, the evidence points to the Defendant."

306. The required typing exam for the job was a pass fail test.
307. The project requires research data analysis skills.
308. The magazine has articles on lifestyle wellness topics.

309. The report states, "The factory fire was caused by human error."
310. The report states: "the factory fire was caused by human error The evidence points to the Defendant."
311. The report states the cause was "by human error. In this case, the evidence points to the Defendant."

Parentheses and Brackets
Exercises for Rules 120 to 125.

Properly use parentheses or brackets in each sentence.

Direct quotation for practice problems:

"Alice was injured in a car accident that month caused by a malfunctioning traffic signal."

Consider a quotation addition as a comment. Consider a quotation change as an important, uncorrected error.

312. Q Did you kill your spouse?
     A Witness shook head side to side.
313. Q Where did you trip and fall on the sidewalk?
     A Witness marked a red X on Exhibit 3.
314. Q Should we take lunch now?
     A Witness nodded head up and down
        Recess from 12:17 p.m. to 1:33 p.m.
315. Mr. Smith testified, "Alice was injured in a car accident that month April 2022 caused by a malfunctioning traffic signal."
316. Mr. Smith's testimony is a repeat of his written statement: "Angela was injured in a car accident."

Italic Formatting
Exercises for Rules 131 to 136.

Properly use italics in each sentence. Consider any foreign word or phrase as unfamiliar unless contained in Rule 133.

317. The movie accurately captured the zeitgeist of the late 1970s.
318. In Roberts v. Pharmco, the plaintiff claimed fraud.

319. For the TV series Home Décor, the latest series on kitchen remodeling is excellent.
320. Do you recommend reading the "Change Yourself" chapter in the bestseller The Best You?
321. The word regimen according to Merriam-Webster's Collegiate Dictionary is defined as "a regular course of action and especially of strenuous training."
322. I searched for the word accident in the deposition and here are the results.
323. The distinction between Crocodylus niloticus and Crocodylus porosus, two species of crocodile, can be challenging for researchers.
324. The Star Trek episode "The Trouble with Tribbles" is a classic.
325. The Judge made an ad hoc decision to change the trial schedule—c'est la vie.
326. The case Counsel is referring to is Lossi v. United States, supra, 532 L.Ed.3d at p. 117.

Capitalization

Fundamental Rules and Work Titles
Exercises for Rules 137 to 139.

Properly capitalize each sentence.

327. the headquarters of intel is in silicon valley.
328. ward stone ireland invented the stenotype in 1911.
329. main street and front street do not intersect.
330. have you read *the history of court reporting in the 1970s*?
331. the golden gate bridge is in the bay area.
332. the officer pursued the suspect's car on elm street.
333. that's a distinctive accent. were you born in arkansas?
334. did I leave my copy of *punctuation for proofreaders* on the table?
335. no, I was born in new orleans near the french quarter.
336. the empire state building is in the big apple.

Titles With a Name
Exercises for Rules 140 to 143.

Properly capitalize each sentence.

337. Did you see captain james roller at the VFW meeting?
338. ted cruz, senator from texas, attended the heated public hearing.
339. I can't believe dad said he was not coming for dinner.
340. Is it true, detective, you found a bloody knife in the trash?
341. Did mayor john anderson, announced a new infrastructure project?
342. The news report showed a clip of gretchen whitmer, governor of michigan, addressing the crowd at the state fair.
343. When is grandpa's medical appointment?

Business, Government, and Court
Exercises for Rules 144 to 150.

Properly capitalize each sentence.

344. I live in the city of sacramento.
345. I got a parking ticket from the city of sacramento.
346. Eve filed a court case that summer.
347. How did the judge rule in *leaf systems inc. v. cook county*?
348. Is the citation in the federal bureau of investigation's report a federal or state law?
349. Is the case with the grand jury or the washoe county superior court?
350. Can bailiff lee please position himself behind counsel and the plaintiff.

Days, Nationalities, and Terms
Exercises for Rules 151 to 163.

Properly capitalize each sentence.

351. Did james roller, captain of the 103rd infantry division, attend the VFW meeting?
352. Did you visit your mom during christmas vacation?

353. Last june, I filed a claim in hoover county superior court.
354. The hoover city council meets wednesdays.
355. The best time to buy a toyota prius is in january.
356. The worst time to buy a dodge truck is in july.
357. Is tylenol or ibuprofen better for a toothache?
358. When I lived with randy, he insisted on using only charmin toilet paper.
359. Does new year's eve fall on a wednesday or thursday this year?
360. Does the defendant understand english or spanish?
361. The suspect was described as either hispanic or caucasian.
362. Did you see amir sitting on a city of miami park bench reading the qur'an?
363. Was antonio, a jehovah's witness, able to buy the latest edition of the *new world translation* of the bible?
364. When I lived in los angeles on the west coast, it took me 90 minutes to drive to work. now I only drive 5 minutes west of my home.
365. The exam had only one essay problem: describe the similarities of battle of bunker hill during the revolutionary war and the battle of the bulge during the second world war.
366. Like the industrial revolution for manufacturing and transportation, the space race and cold war during the twentieth century fueled advancements in science and technology.
367. jane seymore, doctor of physics, was nominated for the davisson-germer prize in 2019.
368. Taking time off to treat my spouse's addison's disease is covered by the americans with disabilities act.
369. I drove nonstop heading southeast from my house in ohio, in the midwest, to alabama, in the south.

Number Formatting

Writing With Words or Figures
Exercises for Rules 164 to 170.

Properly write or correct the number format in each sentence.

370. I only have three pairs of tennis shoes.
371. I have over one hundred books in my personal library.

372. Amanda owns fourteen vintage cars.
373. Do you really own eleven dogs and two cats?
374. Two hundred three small earthquakes were recorded in California last year.
375. No. I have two dogs and nine cats.
376. The library's address ends with two 7's.
377. Oregon's population in nineteen seventy-three was two point two million.
378. Is the two thousand twenty city population found on page one thousand one hundred seventy-three?
379. The U.S. national debt is expected to exceed thirty-four trillion dollars this year.
380. Is the city project estimated at $775,000 or $1.1 million?
381. Did 3 squirrels ran across the road?
382. 25 out of the 4500 ballots were received.
383. One hundred nine new bird species have been cataloged in the last twelve years.
384. One-U is the listed apartment number.
385. We should expect temperatures in the nineties this summer.

Formatting a Date or Time
Exercises for Rules 171 to 175.

Properly write or correct the time or date format in each sentence.

386. The accident occurred on June 5 2020.
387. Did the accident occur on 5 June 2022?
388. Sue's birthday is August twenty-three nineteen ninety-five.
389. Did you go Friday October 11 2021 to her younger brother's birthday?
390. The accident occurred on June 5th 2023 along Hillsdale Drive.
391. The accident occurred on five June 2023 along Hillsdale Drive.
392. The accident occurred in June two thousand twenty-three along Hillsdale Drive.
393. I left work at five ten pm.
394. Do you leave for work at seventeen hundred hours?
395. I set my alarm clock for six-fifteen am.
396. I set my alarm clock for six am

397. I set my alarm clock for six.
398. I set my alarm clock for zero six hundred hours.
399. The morning commute traffic starts at 6 o'clock.
400. I leave for work at 5:00 o'clock when it's still dark.
401. The accident occurred on June 5th two thousand nineteen at about seven thirty in the morning.
402. The accident occurred in June two thousand nineteen at about 7 o'clock in the morning.
403. Was the incident date December eleventh two thousand twenty-three or was it November twelfth two thousand twenty-three?
404. The incident date was actually October eleventh two thousand twenty-three at twelve-fourteen pm.

Formatting a Monetary Amount or Address
Exercises for Rules 176 and 177.

Properly write or correct the monetary amount or address format in each sentence.

405. The car repair bill totaled about eight hundred dollars.
406. Wow, I only paid six hundred fifty dollars for the same car repair.
407. Amy handed me ten dollars and twenty-five cents.
408. Did Dori give you a twenty dollar bill?
409. What happened to the other seventy-five cents?
410. She bought a candy bar for seventy-five cents and gave me fifteen dollars and thrity-five cents.
411. My mailing address is thirteen-thirteen fifty-fifth avenue woodside california 94062.
412. My previous address was one mills street new york.
413. Did Tim buy that motorcycle for ten thousand dollars?
414. No. He bought it for eight thousand.
415. What did Tim do with the spare two thousand dollars?
416. He purchased new tires for three hundred or four hundred dollars.
417. Tim also repaid his mom two hundred dollars. I believe the exact amount was one hundred ninety-two dollars and seventy-five cents.
418. Our company's headquarters are at two hundred forty-six park avenue suite six hundred Dallas Texas 75201.

419. Her childhood home was at five hundred sixty-seven elm street Denver.
420. For every returned check, there is a twenty-nine dollar and ninety-five cent fee.
421. Did you see the soup on sale for ninety-nine cents each?
422. Yes. That's a savings of about one dollar and fifty cents each.
423. Buy a dozen and save eighteen dollars.
424. The conference will take place at three thrity-three convention center boulevard Las Vegas Nevada eight-nine-one-oh-nine.
425. The office is located at one thirteenth street suite four-oh-five Chicago Illinois six-zero-six-zero-one.

Formatting an Ordinal, Percentage, or Fraction
Exercises for Rules 178 to 182.

Properly write or correct the number format in each sentence.

426. I bought eight acres of my parents' property or 10% of what they own.
427. Was Ron eight years old at the time?
428. My height is five feet, eight inches.
429. The new law needs a two thirds majority to pass.
430. The survey showed five eighths of students need financial aid.
431. The cut was three thirty-seconds of an inch deep.
432. I failed the quiz. I only got four tenths of the questions correct.
433. The second step in the chemistry experiment is to add point three ounces of water.
434. I placed ninth in the speed competition.
435. Did Morgan place tenth or eleventh in the speed competition?
436. The room is ten feet by fifteen feet: one hundred fifty square feet.
437. The new 4% fee and 8% tax compounds to a twelve point three percent increase.
438. Is your 10-year-old son in the 4th or 5th grade?
439. I just measured the grain silo level and it is four fifths full.
440. Babe Ruth's batting average was three forty-two.

Miscellaneous Number Formatting
Exercises for Rules 183 to 191.

Properly write or correct the number format in each sentence.

441. My height is six feet, two inches; my brother is six three.
442. Thirteen times thirteen is one hundred sixty-nine.
443. The policy in question is section four paragraph twelve.
444. A detailed timeline of the incident can be found on pages two hundred eighty-five to two hundred ninety-one.
445. My phone number is 777.111.2222.
446. My social security number is 3-3-3-0-0-1-1-1-1.
447. For question number forty-nine, three hundred dollars was stolen, not two hundred fifty dollars.
448. The recipe called for an eight to six ratio of oranges to lemons.
449. I am quoting from page one hundred three line nine.
450. There were thirty odd students in the classroom when the fire alarm went off.
451. The scientific discoveries of the 17th century laid the foundation for modern science.
452. Please refer to article roman numeral eleven section three for clarification.
453. Sarah spent ten some odd minutes looking for her misplaced keys.
454. The manufacturing process is described on page twenty-three figure two.
455. During 2020 to 2022, the economic effects of the U.S. pandemic totaled an estimated four trillion dollars.
456. Is your work telephone number (333) 456 9999 extension 123?
457. Is your social security number really 777777777?
458. World War II occurred during the nineteen-forties.
459. We need to review chapter roman numeral eight for the exam.
460. The novel was one hundred fifty something pages long.

Abbreviation

Exercises for Rules 192 to 197.

Properly write the abbreviations in each sentence.

461. The us national debt per taxpayer is $260,000.
462. The Greek Battle of Marathon occurred in 490 bc.
463. Is it true, Doctor Cooper, that you failed to perform a complete examination?
464. How many local ceo's attended the city budget meeting?
465. Doctor Bell, D.D.S., has been my dentist for 20 years.
466. The report states, "approximate vehicle speed: 45 MPH."
467. Miss Anderson, C.E.O., married Mister Smith Senior, Ph.D.
468. How many tv's do you have in your home, Mister Jones?
469. OK. Did you steal the money, jewelry, etc.?
470. I told the 911 operator to come asap.
471. The C.I.A.s case files are under tight security.
472. Did you hear about doctor j and her groundbreaking research in medicine?
     Note: "J" is an abbreviation of an actual name.
473. The Defendant has five known a.k.a.(s).
474. N.A.S.A.s recent discovery generated excitement in the scientific community.
475. Mister x will be the C.E.O of the company.
     Note: "x" is not an abbreviation of an actual name.

General Practice

General Practice 1:
Properly format and punctuate each sentence.

476. Logan suddenly left his job because 1 poor pay 2 poor management and 3 long commute.
477. I left my trash cans out too long and got a fifty dollar fine from the city of New York.
478. Isabella passed the final speed test, she and her boy friend went out to dinner.
479. I saw the car in the corner of my eye at the last second, unfortunately I was unable to avoid the collision.
480. Did Liam ask what shall we do tonight for dinner?

481. The defendant was id'ed in the police lineup by emma.
482. The crack in the wind shield measured seven-sixteenths of an inch across.
483. According to our records the date of loss is September fifth 2018.
484. The detained teens included a thirteen, fifteen, and seventeen year old.
485. I cannot believe jackson likes cooked carrots and if you can believe this he also likes other vegetables.
486. Sophia was tardy wasn't she to the best of your knowledge to work each day?
487. Punctuation mastery is a life long journey.
488. My mother called my about the situation, the water heater stopped working and there is no hot water.
489. Did mister pearson file a claim in lake county superior court?
490. Did you sell the classic 57 chevy at the car auction in may 2017?
491. I took aspirin for my headache isn't tylenol better?
492. The probation officer reported that he contacted a male and female living at the recently added address in the old case file that the couple stated they are renters who had moved into the home in either june or july of 2018 and that james had not stopped by to see them or been seen in the area for a long time.
493. The poorly constructed deck cost me five thousand dollars to remove and rebuild.
494. I bought several tomato sauce cans for sixty cents each and saved two dollars.
495. Riley Walker lieutenant in the salvation army helped organize the winter clothing drive.
496. Amy responded I know my rights and plan to exercise them.
497. To my daughters catholic baptism I invited Zoe my spiritual advisor, Silas my accountant for ten years, and Rose my closest friend.
498. The sun city pedestrian committee has a no nonsense attitude even on light hearted matters.
499. My lawyers advice is to take the fifteen year deal.
500. Wyatt minds his p's and q's well for a third grade student.

General Practice 2:
Properly format and punctuate each sentence.

501. The question is this - how was your week long trip to Hawaii?
502. Well I own - truth be told - twelve dogs and three cats.
503. Did you add point eight ounces of vanilla extract, did it taste as you hoped?
504. The flight took off at four o'clock in the morning and it landed at seven-fifteen am.
505. Mia passed the mid-term didn't she?
506. The question is why not attend the conference?
507. I mailed the check however I forgot to sign it.
508. Did miss Robinson President of PharmCo announced the stock split?
509. Speak louder please.
510. While in the big apple I stayed in a small quaint hotel near times square.
511. THE COURT we will recess for lunch until one pm.
512. The exam results won't be available until friday - alex remarked.
513. Lucas wrote sophia a love poem - hence he loves her.
514. Ashley my room-mate forgot to set the alarm clock for five forty-five.
515. Please give the 100 page document to the bailiff mister jones.
516. The estimated cost to repair the bridge is between eight hundred thousand dollars and one million two hundred thousand dollars.
517. I booked the meeting room for one-thirty pm and if you cancel for any reason there will be a two hundred dollar fee.
518. We selected a cute cuddly puppy from the shelter.
519. Twenty seven of every twenty million factory produced toys are defective.
520. Cora lived with her sister, didn't she per your prior testimony, before she met and moved in with rebecca?
521. No I failed to pay the rent by five.
522. Every court reporting student needs practice time perseverance etc. to reach the goal of writing two hundred twenty-five words per minute.

523. I like practicing - to be completely honest I love capturing the spoken word.
524. Objection - vague and leading.
525. Hannah loaned you twenty dollars last saturday correct?
526. I did not want to be home alone but everyone I called didn't answer.
527. Ethan dropped his wallet some where - have you seen it?
528. State and spell your full name mister Bell for the record please.
529. After dinner last night with miss cook, margaret said I plan to move to houston this Summer.
530. I plan to move to houston said miss cook after dinner. I have worked with my current employer since November 2020.
531. I worked fulltime for five days to reform the damaged statue.
532. Attorneys for the plaintiff and the defendant stepped outside to argue off the record not on the record.
533. I packed a lunch for our day hike - peanut butter sandwiches chips and bottled water.
534. Mason and ava married on january sixteenth 2018 in seattle washington - do you recall that day?
535. They gave us verbal approval to purchase the new tires - unfortunately the amount exceeded their credit limit.
536. The museum opens doesn't it at ten am on tuesdays?
537. Did you include the December January and February business purchases in the expense report?
538. Yes I included those months in the decision making report.
    Note: Base punctuation on Exercise 537.
539. No all the broad based data was not available at the time.
    Note: Base punctuation on Exercise 537.
540. Alice mentioned that she was at work yesterday but every one I asked didn't see her.
541. While punctuating transcripts I had a light bulb moment not to dilly dally.
542. Womens clothing is more expensive than mens clothing – why is that?
543. OK after you received the call your eta was five minutes right?

544. My next available appointment times are monday one-thirty pm, tuesday eleven-thirty am, and wednesday three pm.
545. Peanut butter sandwiches; chips and bottled water I packed a lunch for our day hike.
546. There is a mistake in figure number four; page thirty-seven.
547. I mailed the package on monday - in fact I mailed it around twelve-fifteen during my lunch break.
548. My last name is spelled S a k s double i.
549. Because the discrepancy is over ten thousand dollars it is prioritized and called high risk.
550. Is labor day in may or september - I always mix up that holiday with memorial day.

General Practice 3:
Properly format and punctuate each sentence.

551. Margaret you can never practice too much right?
552. I cannot make the appointment, I have a hearing in Superior Court.
553. All right I must clear this with the presidents secretary.
554. I went to the store and bought milk eggs bread.
555. I recently bought twelve apple computers for my business and I own one apple computer at home too.
556. I have been to the eiffel tower and while I was in france I took over one hundred fifty photographs.
557. Is it true that doctor cooper of Lower Michigan WeCare Health Care Group examined you in july two thousand twenty-one?
558. I remember july fourth two thousand sixteen as a cool summers day.
559. Nora witnessed the armed robbery - her husband missed it because he ran into a college friend.
560. We were enjoying the movie when someone yelled fire get out.
561. Did you catch the dallas cowboys game last night?
562. I watch what people call nerd tv, shows on comic books and superheroes.
563. Admit it, you returned to the scene of the crime didn't you?

564. 75 gallons of diesel fuel spilled on the roadway after the truck lost control and hit a tree.
565. You speak super fast, are you from the east coast?
566. Zubov vs. Willams is a nineteen fifty-four greene county illinois patent infringement case.
567. Billy has had only one good friend since childhood Lydia.
568. The approved budget for jackson county totals two hundred fourteen million dollars.
569. Anna upon secretly paying the maître d' was immediately seated in the busy restaurant.
570. Who yelled quote unquote fire in the packed restaurant?
571. I believe it was Mark a forty year old man with a tattoo that covers about fifty percent of his arm.
572. Melissa knew it was better to pay twenty dollars for twelve candles rather than two dollars each.
573. My boss harps on the do's and don't's.
574. Only 3 witnesses a bartender a toxicologist and a bar patron were called as witnesses by the defendants attorney.
575. Molly got on the old fashioned bus didn't she for the down town city tour?
576. She refused to agree to the contract terms unless adam did one thing apologize for his short sighted behavior.
577. Did caleb take the wrong coat by mistake or did he take it without asking - do you know?
578. I tracked my package online as it went through nashville tennessee, st louis missouri, and wichita kansas.
579. Tom how many s-es are in dessert?
580. Did your wife have the youngest daughter at home 2398 5th avenue wilwaukee wisconsin.
581. No our daughter was born at the hospital and the attending physician was doctor albert torre.
     Note: Base punctuation on Exercise 581.
582. Unfortunately the two hour tennis match was not an action packed event.
583. Broken glass; twisted metal and dripping radiator fluid debris littered the fresh crash site.
584. A woman rushed to a heavily damaged car and asked the driver are you OK?
585. The driver moaned you're an angel aren't you?

586. Scott dreamed of only thing for 3 consecutive nights the delivery person would finally arrive with his new stenograph steno machine.
587. When I started the car the stereo volume was on maximum but james my son who last drove the car denies crankin it up.
588. The stereo speaker however was damaged and needed to be repaired - unfortunately my son didn't have the money to fix it.
589. As a result, my son got a parttime decent earning job to pay the repair bill of three hundred forty-nine dollar and ninety-five cents.
590. Keith my son needed to work only two months and he paid the repair bill.
591. Sadie and ava went ice skating together yet neither of them knew how to ice skate.
592. Their friends debated if ice skating was a worst case or best case situation for them.
593. Upon arriving at the ice rink they took a free beginners class.
594. The beginners class was divided into no, little, and some experience groups.
595. Paul stone junior ph.d. founded the high tech firm in 1986.
596. I can arrange a meeting with mister stone this afternoon but if you are not available I can see if mister stone can meet tomorrow at eight am.
597. Mister stone is not available tomorrow friday at 9 o'clock correct?
598. No mister stone is a nice friendly guy and his schedule is generally full.
      Note: Base punctuation on Exercise 597.
599. Has evan read the recent article, free time, in the new york times – it's in section D, page five?
600. Yes she read it - you should read "twenty five hours a day" a book the author wrote in 2019.
      Note: Base punctuation on Exercise 599.

Answer Key

Grammar: Identifying an Independent or Dependent Clause
1. (Everyone was busy), and (I went to the movie alone).
2. (I will see) [if the book has arrived].
3. (Mary needs to check back tomorrow) [before the store opens].
4. (I'm counting calories), but (I really want dessert).
5. (Cats are good pets) [because they are clean].
6. (Tommy dragged a chair across the wood floor) [while his mother watched in horror].
7. (Tommy, [who is 11 years old], was scolded by his mother).
8. (The mistake [that you made] will be corrected).
9. (I don't know) [where the keys are].
10. (Her mom was pleased) [when she got the job].
11. [As you read the textbook], (you will find the answers) [that you are looking for].
12. (He ran out of money), yet (he didn't stop playing poker).
13. (I drove to school with a friend).
14. (I dove my car) [that recently got new brakes].
15. (I do not know) [how far it is to school].
16. (Mary lives one floor above you).
17. (Our secretary, [who is never late], called in sick at 9:00 a.m.)
18. (I do not know) [who gave you the flu].
19. (The client said) [that he would call us next week].
20. [When he calls], (tell him our rates have slightly increased).

Grammar: Identifying a Coordinating Conjunction, Conjunctive Adverb, Transitional Expression, or Parenthetical Expression
21. Everyone was busy, (and) I went to the movie alone.
22. Sally didn't want to go to the dentist; [therefore], she canceled.
23. He ran out of money, (yet) he didn't stop playing poker.
24. I lost my job. [Consequently], my car was repossessed.
25. I left 30 minutes early; [however], an accident still made me late.
26. [To tell you the truth], I hate Monday mornings.
27. I saw the suspect. [In fact], I can recall what he was wearing.

Grammar: Identifying a Prepositional or Verbal Phrase

28. Don't step (on the broken glass).
29. [Seeing his excellent test score], he fainted.
30. The dog jump (in the car).
31. The book (on the table) is now missing.
32. [To provide a safe work environment], security cameras were installed.
33. Robert lives (in the apartment) (around the corner).
34. [Strong-minded to get the cookies (on top of the refrigerator)], Tommy dragged a chair (across the floor).

Grammar: Determining an Essential or Nonessential Element

35. A man (who wore black) is the suspect.
36. Brandon, [who wore black], is the suspect.
    Note: The element is likely nonessential.
37. The officer arrived in a black and white car, [a patrol car].
38. The Defendant, [Mr. Smith], hired a private attorney.
    Note: Answer assumes there is only one defendant.
39. A psychologist (Dr. Cooper) is highly respected.
40. Amber's psychologist, [Dr. Cooper], is highly respected.
    Note: Answer assumes Amber has only one psychologist.

The Period

41. I passed the test.
42. I passed the test. We went out to dinner.
43. Please speak up.
44. Can you state and spell your full name for the record.
45. I object. The question is beyond the scope.
46. Objection. The question is vague.
47. Objection. Ambiguous. Compound.
48. Hurry. We're going to be late.
49. Crap. I don't know.
50. All right. Fine. We can take a recess now.

The Comma: Introductory Phrase or Clause

51. To provide a safe work environment, security cameras were installed.
52. On reaching Nevada, we stopped at the first place we could gamble.
53. Running out of money, he didn't stop playing poker.
54. On the concrete sidewalk, our dog sat obediently.

55. To tell you the truth, I hate Monday mornings.
56. Across the street, a squirrel darted with a nut.
57. Because they are clean, cats are good pets.
58. In 2018, 91 people graduated from the small elementary school.
59. He said he was not in town yesterday. However, many people saw him.
60. While his mother watched in horror, Tommy dragged a chair across the wood floor.

The Comma: Compound or Complex Sentence
61. I lost my job last week, and my car was repossessed.
62. I'm counting calories, but I really want dessert.
63. Linda was telling the truth, or she was telling a huge lie.
64. Everyone was busy, so I went to the movie alone.
65. He ran out of money, yet he didn't stop playing poker.
66. The dentist, but he went anyway.
       Or: The dentist. But he
67. I worked ten days last month, yet able to pay the rent.
68. You should tell the whole story, or face the consequences.
69. He said he was not in town yesterday, but recognizing his obvious lie, he made up a cover story.
70. Tammy could not decide what to do, and to tell you the truth, she had to slept on it.

The Comma: Series of Items
71. I need to buy milk and bread. [No comma]
72. I need to buy milk, eggs, and bread.
73. I need to buy milk, eggs, bread.
74. I need to buy milk and eggs and bread. [No commas]
75. Please invite John, Sue, Liam, and Sarah to the meeting.
76. A court reporting student needs a steno machine, a computer, the textbooks, et cetera.
77. A court reporting student needs to buy the textbook, the workbook, a notebook, et cetera before the first day of instruction.
       Gregg: a notebook, et cetera, before the
78. Did you mail the invitations and response cards and directions to the guests? [no commas]
79. Did you mail the invitations, response cards, and directions to the guests?

80. Did you mail the case file to Mr. Smith at Clark, Garcia, Jones & Smith?

The Comma: Nonessential Element, Interrupting Element, or Participle Phrase.
81. He said that he was not in town yesterday. Many people, however, saw him.
82. Mary Sue, who is my half sister, was born in 1994.
83. I, upon arriving at the accident scene, fainted at the sight of blood.
84. It happened, you know, right after, like, dinner.
85. The original document was important, containing the first photograph of the accident scene.
86. The motion, filed just yesterday with the Court, was immediately denied by the judge.
87. I don't like the looks of this, to tell you the truth.
88. My situation, in so many words, is bad.
89. NewLeaf Recycling, which started in this city 15 years ago, is relocating to Chicago.
90. Janet shouted the answer, bursting with confidence.

The Comma: Contrasting Phrase, Direct Address, or Coordinate Adjective
91. I briskly walk, never jog, one hour each day.
92. I said Mr. Ogawa, not Mrs. Ogawa.
93. It will be another hot, windy day.
94. His cruel, callous actions demanded a severe sentence.
95. The old ghost town is not on the map. [no comma]
96. The smart, charismatic employee quickly promoted to shift manager.
97. Please approach the bench, Ms. Anderson.
98. Explain what you mean, sir, by "gently used"?
99. The attorneys conferred off the record, not on the record.
100. Please speak up, ma'am.

The Comma: Title or Degree with a Personal Name; Jr. or Sr.; an Appositive; or an Enumeration
101. Did Dr. Smith, your primary care physician, see you last week?
102. The tree, tall and strong, withstood the strong winds.
103. Dr. Jones, of South Carolina Family Healthcare Group, is my physical therapist.

37

104. Did you invite Melody Jones, Esq., to the briefing?
105. Katy Banks, PhD, is schedule to testify on Tuesday.
106. Ron Davies Jr. is also attending the briefing. [no commas]
    Or (person prefers commas): Ron Davies, Jr., is
107. Did you hear Mr. Jones III died last week? [no commas]
108. Did you know William Jones Sr. founded the law firm?
    Or (person prefers commas): William Jones, Sr., founded
109. What gifts do I want? First, a gift certificate to Ulta. Beauty. Second, dinner at my favorite restaurant.
110. Make sure to include the following on your application: one, a contact email; two, the best time to call you; and, three, a contact email.

The Comma: Yes and No
111. Yes, I do.
112. I do not, no.
113. I work for the County of Santa Clara. No.

114. Yes. She left with James around 4:30 p.m.
115. I worked until 5:00 p.m. that day. No.
116. No, I did not see her leave.

117. No, I was not speeding.
118. No. I was driving about 35 miles per hour.
119. The posted speed limit is 35. No.
120. I was not, no.

The Comma: the Words *Please, Too, Including, Such As,* or *Like*; and *Inc.* or *LLC* in a Business Name
121. Darn, I spilled coffee on my pants.
122. Now, let's move on to the next problem.
123. Will you please turnoff your cell phone. [no comma]
124. Will you turnoff you cell phone, please.
125. He's not just an actor; he's a singer too. [no comma]
126. She, too, enjoys swimming.
127. The zoo has a variety of animals, such as lions and elephants.
128. We visited famous landmarks including the Eiffel Tower and the Colosseum. [no comma]
    Or (if deemed nonessential): landmarks, including
129. Tech Solutions Inc. organized the conference. [no comma]
    Or (company uses commas): Solutions, Inc., organized

130. Tech Solutions Inc.—for the first time since the pandemic—organized the conference. [no comma]
    Or (company uses commas): Solutions, Inc.—for

The Semicolon: Compound Sentences
131. Richard does not like broccoli; he hates it.
    Or: like broccoli. He hates
132. My father's ancestors are from Germany; my mother's ancestors are from England.
    Or: from Germany. My mother's
133. I saw James in the corner of my eye; unfortunately, I did not see which direction he went.
    Or: my eye. Unfortunately, I did
134. I did my homework; however, I did the wrong set of problems.
    Or: homework. However, I did
135. Ashley was the only person who could make the decision; therefore, she weighed the evidence carefully.
    Or: decision. Therefore, she
136. She weighed the evidence; as a result, the decision was sound.
    Or: evidence. As a result, the decision
137. I told the truth; as I see it, I told the whole truth.
    Or: truth. As I see it, I told
138. I like him; to be honest, I love him.
    Or: him. To be honest, I
139. I saw the accident; my husband saw nothing.
    Or: the accident. My husband
140. I saw James in the corner of my eye; thus I did not see which direction he went.
    Or: my eye. Thus I did
141. I bought a new 15-inch laptop, cell phone, and tablet; and I planned to set them up over the holiday weekend.
    Or (avoid): and tablet. And I planned
    Not: and tablet, and I planned
142. As I entered the room, I noticed the lights flickering; and if I had not left immediately, I would be in the dark.
    Not: flickering, and if

143. Jack loves Melissa; in fact, he sent her flowers.
    Or: Melissa. In fact, he
144. Jack sent Melissa flowers; hence he loves her.

Or: flowers. Hence he
145. Jack sent Melissa flowers; however, he forgot the card.
Or: flowers. However, he

The Semicolon: Series of Items
146. The Defendant has lived in New York City, New York; San Francisco, California; and Detroit, Michigan.
147. Please grab the red ring of keys, the car keys; a bottle of water from the refrigerator; and my lunch
Note: "the car keys" is an appositive (Rule 26)
148. I arrived at work at 9:30 a.m.; turned on my computer; and called Denise, the director's secretary.
Note: "the director's secretary is an appositive (Rule 26)
149. The officer stated that he contacted the people living at the address of the complaint given five minutes earlier by **dispatch; that** he talked to the people living at the address about the recent noise complaint of the **party; and that** he advised the people living at the address to turn down the volume on the large stereo system.
Or: dispatch, that . . . party, and that
150. My next available times are Wednesday, 9:00 a.m.; Thursday, 1:30 p.m.; and Friday, 10:30 a.m.
151. The account payments were received on June 9, 2022; July 11, 2022; August 6, 2022; and September 10, 2022.
152. I consulted with my lawyer, Ms. Anderson; my CPA, Mr. Smith; and an expert in the field, Ms. Cooper.
153. I invited Jim, the office manager; Joan, the financial manager; and Linda, the supervisor.

The Semicolon: The Words *For Example*, *Namely*, or *That is*
154. The software comes with several useful features; for example, data encryption. [afterthought]
155. The exhibit features various types of art; namely, paintings, sculptures, and photograph. [list]
Or: of art: namely, painting
156. The project requires specific skills; that is, data analysis and project management are essential. [explanatory clause]
Or: skills: that is, data
157. The instructions are straightforward who to contact in an emergency—namely, the manager. [appositive]
Or: emergency, namely, the manager

158. The recipe calls for a few essential ingredients; namely, flour, sugar, and eggs. [list]
     Or: ingredients: namely, flour

The Semicolon: Enumerated Phrases
159. The reasons for the employment termination were (1) excessive tardiness, (2) substandard work quality, and (3) arguing with other employees.
     Or (not preferred): The reasons for the employment termination were, one, excessive tardiness; two, substandard work quality; and, three, arguing with other employees.
160. I quit my last job because (A) the manager was verbally abusive, (B) better pay, and (C) better benefits.
     Or (not preferred): I quit my last job because, A, the manager was verbally abusive; B, better pay; and, C, better benefits.

The Colon
161. Luke did not know the new law: All bicyclists must wear helmets.
     Note: Capitalize due to statement of a rule (Rule 48)
     Or: new law; all bicyclists
     Or: new law. All bicyclists
162. Amy is afraid of only one bug: spiders.
163. He had his favorite meal that evening: soup, steak, and French fries.
164. The accident report contained one glaring fact: he was traveling well above the speed limit based on the skid marks.
     Or: glaring fact; he was
     Or: glaring fact. He was
165. The following law enforcement agencies were at the scene of the accident: a sheriff, an NYPD officer, and a detective.
166. An attorney advised me about my claim: there was probably not enough evidence to win in court.
     Or: my claim; there was
     Or: my claim. There was

167. THE COURT: Juror No. 5 is dismissed.
168. Susan passed the skills test: Her endless hours of practice paid off.

41

<u>Or</u>: skills test; her endless

<u>Or</u>; skills test. Her endless

169. These are the reasons for the increase in Bay Area home sales: economic recovery and low-interest rates.

170. I want you to understand that I saw a large, hairy thing that night: a Bigfoot.

171. The sign at the construction site states, "Caution: Hard Hat Area."

172. MS. ANDERSON: The witness has not been qualified as an expert.

173. John failed to make the job candidate list: He was just shy of the experience requirement.

    <u>Or</u>: candidate list; he was

    <u>Or</u>: candidate list. He was

174. She had two things on her mind rushing to get ready for work: turn off the iron and remember the case file.

175. We know the reason for the murder: money.

The Dash

176. I took—borrowed the money.

177. I'll be frank with you—mark my words because this is the honest truth—I did not steal the money.

178. Q Did you steal—

    A No.

    Q —the money?

179. Q How long did it take you to recover—

    A Four months.

    Q —from the surgery?

180. The primary defense team—Tom, Sue, and I—was retained on April 2, 2022.

181. The needed food—bread, milk, and cheese—was bought on the way home.

182. Tom, Sue, and I—the primary defense team was retained on April 2, 2022.

183. The need food—strike that. Did you stop on the way home.

184. Q Were you speeding—

    A I need a break.

    Q After this question—at the time of the accident?

        <u>Or</u>: Q After this question.

—at the time of the accident?
185. Did you buy—correction—stop on the way home?

The Question Mark
186. She's right, isn't she?
187. He proposed to you Saturday evening, correct?
188. There were two suspects, wasn't there, in the vehicle?
189. The children were excited, were they not, that Christmas morning?
190. You were headed southbound—is that not correct?—during the evening commute?
191. Were two suspects in the vehicle? I'm talking about after you witnessed the robbery?
192. You were headed southbound? Is that a good statement?
193. The defendant wore a blue jacket. Do you remember?
194. You were headed southbound. Isn't that correct?
195. She drove, didn't she, southbound?
196. You have never lived in a big city, have you?
197. I'm right, am I not, that you've only lived out in the country?
198. You have only lived out in the country, right?
199. What I asked was, Did you date the Plaintiff in 2021?
200. The question is simple this: where were you that day?
201. You were headed southbound. Do you remember?
202. Was his coat red? White? Blue?
      Or: Was his coat red? White? blue?
203. Did you ever think, How is my father doing after his hip replacement?
204. What were you doing before the accident? Using the cell phone?
205. My last question was, You saw Dr. Cooper on January 11, 2018?

Quotation Mark: Punctuation Marks
206. Freddie screamed, "fire." [period incorrect]
207. "Let's go out for dinner," Rory said. [comma incorrect]
208. Linda turned the TV to a "nature show": a shark feeding frenzy. [colon incorrect]
209. Tom said, "grab one"; "grab what," Mindy responded. [semicolon and second comma incorrect]
210. Susan asked, "Are you feeling lucky today?"

[comma missing and question mark incorrect]
211. "I'm flying to Detroit," Tom signed. "You go where the work is." [comma and second period incorrect]

Quotation Mark: Direct Quotations
212. The officer said, "Drop it."
213. She replied, "I'm going to quit this job if I don't get a raise."
214. James said, "I'll drop it off on my way home."
215. "Put your hands on your head," the officer instructed.
216. "I got the job," I squealed.
217. The police report states, "At 3:17 p.m., a stolen-car call was received."
    Or: report states: "At 3:17 p.m. [consistent usage]
218. The code section stipulates, "All persons shall give a notice of 30 days."
    Or: section stipulates: "All persons [consistent usage]
219. "Don't hit your brother," Tammy said sternly. "You must learn to share."
220. "I'm going to quit this job," she replied, "if I don't get a raise."
221. Rachel asked, "What do you want for dinner tonight?"
222. Did Rachel ask, "What do you want for dinner tonight?"
223. Did Angela say, "I'm making spaghetti for dinner"?
224. The officer said, quote, "Drop it," unquote.
    Not: The officer said, quote, Drop it, unquote.
    Not: The officer said, "Drop it."
225. William replied, quote/unquote, "I quit."
    Not: William replied, quote/unquote, I quit.
    Not: William replied, "I quit."
226. The code section states, quote, "All persons shall give a notice of 30 days."
    Or: states, quote: "All persons [consistent usage]
227. The report stated the important detail on page 3: "At 3:17 p.m., a stolen-car call was received."
    Not: on page 3, "At 3:17 [see Rule 75]
228. The officer was forceful in his instructions: "Drop it."
229. Peter said, "I don't understand the detailed instructions."
230. Amy responded, "I know the laws in this state."
231. "I could not tell you," Tim responded, "what Andrew's problem is."
232. "The tax on the car is over $3,000," Randy gasped.

44

233. I think the suspect said, quote, "Give me your wallet," close quote.
    <u>Not</u>: said, quote, Give me your wallet, close quote
    <u>Not</u>: said, "Give me your wallet."
234. Did the suspect say, quote/unquote, "Give me your wallet"?
    <u>Not</u>: say, quote/unquote, Give me your wallet?
    <u>Not</u>: say, "Give me your wallet"?
235. Deborah asked, "How much did it cost to fix the car?"

Quotation Mark: Titles, Special Emphasis, or *So-Called*

236. The document is titled "Know Your Punctuation."
237. Ann's favorite *Home and Garden* TV show episode is "Backyard Décor."
238. Due to Jack's previous jail escape, he is labeled "high risk."
239. Mr. Wright said he bought a "chopper," a gun, while on parole.
240. The so-called experts failed to predict the current economic situation. [no quotation marks]
    <u>Not</u>: so-called "experts" failed
241. Have you seen the *Star Trek* episode "The Enemy Within"?
242. What did the Defendant, Mr. Smith, mean by "self-help"?
243. To answer your question, I recommend reading "The New You" chapter in the bestseller *Be Your Best*.
244. Success involves hard work; there is no so-called easy route. [no quotation marks]
    <u>Not</u>: no so-called "easy route."

Quotation Mark: Mispronounced or Made-Up Word; Definition or Translation

245. The hilarious joke made me "snickernoodle" with laughter.
246. Amy went nuclear with the comment.
    <u>Note</u>: The mispronunciation is likely unimportant.

247. I met with Charles Sher-bert [phonetic] on October 14.
    <u>Or</u>: with Charles Sherbert on
    <u>Or</u>: with Charles Sherbit on
    [mispronunciation deemed unimportant.]
248. The dictionary defines *zeitgeist* as "the general intellectual, moral, and cultural climate of an era."
249. Did Peter "Yogi" Berra play for the New York Yankees?

The Apostrophe: Singular and Plural Word Possessive
250. Someone stole the plaintiff's purse from the courtroom.
251. Have you seen April's missing wallet?
252. Children's toys are so expensive.
253. My brother-in-law's testimony did not help the case.
254. I want to hear the next two witnesses' testimony.
255. I need to get my boss's approval.
256. The professor's research is groundbreaking.

The Apostrophe: Various Possessive Rules
257. Tom claimed the heavy lifting violated workers' rights.
258. I bought some fresh produce at the farmers' market.
259. The month's gas bill is higher than last months'.
260. The President's speech's main message was unity
261. The homework of my daughter's friend was found stuffed in the backpack's pocket.
262. The storm undid a week's worth of yard work.
263. How do you think the girls' soccer team will do this year?
264. Don't use the boys restroom by mistake.
    <u>Note</u>: *boys* is a descriptive.
265. I gave my two weeks' notice at work.

The Apostrophe: Plural of a Letter or Misread Word; Omission of a Letter or Figure; Certain Verb Forms
266. Is there one or two L's in traveled?
    <u>Or</u> (acceptable, not recommended): two Ls in
267. Each judge has their dos and don'ts
    <u>Merriam-Webster</u>: dos and don'ts
268. I spell my name, Bret, with one t, not two t's.
269. I sold my '68 Ford Mustang.
270. Hana doesn't recall. Her surgery was in either 2017 or '18.
271. Did you say *talkin'* or *walkin'*?
272. Cindy x'd out the spelling mistake and wrote the correction above.

273. Patrick ID'd the suspect handcuffed in the patrol car.
274. I 86'd the junk straight into the trashcan.

The Hyphen: Prefix and Suffix
275. Who won the countywide race in District 2?
276. Were there any postoperative complications?
277. The illegal firearms found in the raid consisted mostly of semiautomatic rifles.
278. The witness corrected his statement and re-marked the exhibit.?
279. I invest in both long- and short-term securities.
280. On Tuesdays, the board has both an open- and closed-door session.
281. I lived on a small co-op until 14 years old.
282. Do you have and pre-Thanksgiving traditions?
283. Focus groups were divided into 20-, 30-, and 40-year-olds.
284. As I recall, I had a hotel room on the twenty-second or -third floor.
285. The fashion was retro: 1970-like.

The Hyphen: Compound Words
286. I once saw a group of zookeepers capture a man-eating alligator.
287. Are there any cross-references for the compound adjective rules in *The Chicago Manual of Style*?
288. Please check the timetable to see what time the bus arrives.
289. I was shortchanged by the cashier.
290. Did you have your suit dry-cleaned before the start of the trial?
291. A high-level meeting was scheduled after the annual budget was not approved.
292. I feared a worst-case situation: layoffs.
293. However, the bottom-line results were no raises or overtime.
294. This caused a year of penny-pinching purchases and decisions.
295. I hope the budget crisis is not a long-lasting problem.
296. The "are you seriously that freaking stupid" look stopped me cold.
   <u>Or</u>: are-you-seriously-that-freaking-stupid

297. The fast-paced and lopsided football game ended in our favor.
298. The newly formed football team needed more practice.
    Not: newly-formed
299. I received a "how are you doing after all these years?" welcome.
    Or: how-are-you-doing-after-all-these-year?
300. The old coal-mining town is a popular hiking destination.
301. The house used A-frame architecture.
302. Is your position at the law firm full-time or part-time?
303. The X-ray technician X-rayed my arm in four different angles or positions.
    Or: X-ray technician x-rayed
304. My last name is Schmidt, S-c-h-m-i-d-t, not Smith.
305. My name is Staci Green, S-t-a-c-i G-r, double e, n

The Ellipsis and Slash
306. The required typing exam for the job was a pass/fail test.
307. The project requires research / data analysis skills.
308. The magazine has articles on lifestyle/wellness topics.
309. The report states, "The factory fire . . . was caused by human error."
310. The report states: "the factory fire . . . was caused by human error. . . . The evidence points to the Defendant."
311. The report states the cause was ". . . by human error. In this case, the evidence points to the Defendant."

Parentheses and Brackets
312. Q   Did you kill your spouse?
    A   (Witness shook head side to side.)
313. Q   Where did you trip and fall on the sidewalk?
    A   (Witness marked a red X on Exhibit 3.)
314. Q   Should we take lunch now?
    A   (Witness nodded head up and down)
        (Recess from 12:17 p.m. to 1:33 p.m.)
315. Mr. Smith testified, "Alice was injured in a car accident that month [April 2022] caused by a malfunctioning traffic signal."
316. Mr. Smith's testimony is a repeat of his written statement: "Angela [*sic*] was injured in a car accident."
    Or: statement: "Angela [Alice] was

48

Italic Formatting
For clarity, italicized words appear in italics and bold type.

317. The movie accurately captured the **zeitgeist** of the late 1970s.
318. In **Roberts v. Pharmco**, the plaintiff claimed fraud.
319. For the TV series **Home Décor**, the latest series on kitchen remodeling is excellent.
320. Do you recommend reading the "Change Yourself" chapter in the bestseller **The Best You**?
321. The word **regimen** according to **Merriam-Webster's Collegiate Dictionary** is defined as "a regular course of action and especially of strenuous training."
322. I searched for the word **accident** in the deposition and here are the results.
323. The distinction between **Crocodylus niloticus** and **Crocodylus porosus**, two species of crocodile, can be challenging for researchers.
324. The **Star Trek** episode "The Trouble with Tribbles" is a classic.
325. The Judge made an ad hoc decision to change the trial schedule—**c'est la vie**.
    Note: Do not italicize "ad hoc."
326. The case Counsel is referring to is **Lossi v. United States**, **supra**, 532 L.Ed.3d at p. 117.

Capitalization: Fundamental Rules and Work Titles
For clarity, capitalized letters appear in bold type.

327. The headquarters of **I**ntel is in **S**ilicon **V**alley
328. **W**ard **S**tone **I**reland invented the **S**tenotype in 1911.
    Note: *Stenotype* refers to a specific shorthand machine.
329. **M**ain **S**treet and **F**ront **S**treet do not intersect.
330. Have you read *The History of Court Reporting in the 1970s*?
331. The **G**olden **G**ate **B**ridge is in the **B**ay **A**rea.
332. The officer pursued the suspect's car on **E**lm **S**treet.
333. That's a distinctive accent. **W**ere you born in **A**rkansas?
334. **D**id I leave my copy of *Punctuation for Proofreaders* on the table?
335. **N**o, I was born in **N**ew **O**rleans near the **F**rench **Q**uarter.
336. The **E**mpire **S**tate **B**uilding is in the **B**ig **A**pple.

Capitalization: Titles With a Name
For clarity, capitalized letters appear in bold type.

337. Did you see **C**aptain **J**ames **R**oller at the VFW meeting?
338. **T**ed **C**ruz, senator from **T**exas, attended the heated public hearing.
339. I can't believe **D**ad said he was not coming for dinner.
340. Is it true, **D**etective, you found a bloody knife in the trash?
341. Did **M**ayor **J**ohn **A**nderson, announced a new infrastructure project?
342. The news report showed a clip of **G**retchen **W**hitmer, governor of **M**ichigan, addressing the crowd at the state fair.
343. When is **G**randpa's medical appointment?

Capitalization: Business, Government, and Court
For clarity, capitalized letters appear in bold type.

344. I live in the city of **S**acramento.
345. I got a parking ticket from the **C**ity of **S**acramento.
346. Eve filed a court case that summer. [no capitalization]
347. How did the judge rule in *Leaf Systems Inc. v. Cook County*?
348. Is the citation in the **F**ederal **B**ureau of **I**nvestigation's report a federal or state law?
349. Is the case with the grand jury or the **W**ashoe **C**ounty **S**uperior **C**ourt?
     <u>Acceptable</u> (if short form): the **G**rand **J**ury or
350. Can **B**ailiff **L**ee please position himself behind **C**ounsel and the **D**efendant.

Capitalization: Days, Nationalities, and Terms
For clarity, capitalized letters appear in bold type.

351. Did **J**ames **R**oller, captain of the 103rd **I**nfantry **D**ivision, attend the VFW meeting?
352. Did you visit your mom during **C**hristmas vacation?
353. Last **J**une, I filed a claim in **H**oover **C**ounty **S**uperior **C**ourt.
354. The **H**oover **C**ity **C**ouncil meets **W**ednesdays.
355. The best time to buy a **T**oyota **P**rius is in **J**anuary.
356. The worst time to buy a **D**odge truck is in **J**uly.

357. Is **T**ylenol or ibuprofen better for a toothache?
358. When I lived with **R**andy, he insisted on using only **C**harmin toilet paper.
359. Does **N**ew **Y**ear's **E**ve fall on a **W**ednesday or **T**hursday this year?
360. Does the **D**efendant understand **E**nglish or **S**panish?
361. The suspect was described as either **H**ispanic or **C**aucasian.
362. Did you see **A**mir sitting on a city of **M**iami park bench reading the **Q**ur'an?
363. Was **A**ntonio, a **J**ehovah's **W**itness, able to buy the latest edition of the *New World Translation* of the **B**ible?
364. When I lived in **L**os **A**ngeles on the **W**est **C**oast, it took me 90 minutes to drive to work. **N**ow I only drive 5 minutes west of my home.
365. The exam had only one essay problem: describe the similarities of **B**attle of **B**unker **H**ill during the **R**evolutionary **W**ar and the **B**attle of the **B**ulge during the **S**econd **W**orld **W**ar.
366. Like the **I**ndustrial **R**evolution for manufacturing and transportation, the **S**pace **R**ace and **C**old **W**ar during the twentieth century fueled advancements in science and technology.
367. Jane **S**eymore, **D**octor of **P**hysics, was nominated for the **D**avisson-**G**ermer **P**rize in 2019.
368. Taking time off to treat my spouse's **A**ddison's disease is covered by the **A**mericans with **D**isabilities **A**ct.
369. I drove nonstop heading southeast from my house in **O**hio, in the **M**idwest, to **A**labama, in the **S**outh.

Numbers: Writing with Words or Figures
370. I only have three pairs of tennis shoes. [no correction]
371. I have over 100 books in my personal library.
      <u>Acceptable</u> (de-emphasis): one hundred
372. Amanda owns 14 vintage cars.
373. Do you really own 11 dogs and 2 cats?
374. 203 small earthquakes were recorded in California last year.
375. No. I have two dogs and nine cats. [no correction]
376. The library's address ends with two 7s.
377. Oregon's population in 1973 was 2.2 million.
378. Is the 2020 city population found on page 1103?

379. The U.S. national debt is expected to exceed $34 trillion this year.
380. Is the city project estimated at $775,000 or $1,100,000?
381. Did three squirrels ran across the road?
382. Twenty-five out of the 4,500 ballots were received.
383. 109 new bird species have been cataloged in the last 12 years.
384. 1U is the listed apartment number.
385. We should expect temperatures in the 90s this summer.

Numbers: Formatting a Date or Time
386. The accident occurred on June 5, 2020.
387. Did the accident occur on 23 May 2022? [no correction]
388. Sue's birthday is August 23, 1995.
389. Did you go Friday, October 11, 2021, to her younger brother's birthday?
390. The accident occurred on June 5, 2023, along Hillsdale Drive.
391. The accident occurred on 5 June 2023 along Hillsdale Drive.
392. The accident occurred in June 2023 along Hillsdale Drive.
393. I left work at 5:10 p.m.
394. Do you leave for work at 1700 hours?
395. I set my alarm clock for 6:15 a.m.
396. I set my alarm clock for 6:00 a.m.
    Acceptable: 6 a.m.
397. I set my alarm clock for 6:00.
    Acceptable: for six. [no correction]
398. I set my alarm clock for 0600 hours.
399. The morning commute traffic starts at six o'clock.
    Acceptable: 6 o'clock [no correction]
400. I leave for work at five o'clock when it's still dark.
    Acceptable: 5 o'clock
401. The accident occurred on June 5, 2019, at about 7:30 in the morning.
402. The accident occurred in June 2019 at about seven o'clock in the morning.
    Acceptable: 7 o'clock
403. Was the incident date December 11, 2023, or was it November 12, 2023?
404. The incident date was actually October 11, 2023, at 12:14 p.m.

Numbers: Formatting a Monetary Amount or Address

405. The car repair bill totaled about $800.
406. Wow, I only paid $650 for the same car repair.
407. Amy handed me $10.25.
408. Did Dori give you a $20 bill?
409. What happened to the other 75 cents?
410. She bought a candy bar for $0.75 and gave me $15.35.
411. My mailing address is 1313 55th Avenue, Woodside, California 94062.
412. My previous address was 1 Mills Street, New York.
     Acceptable: One Mills Street
413. Did Tim buy that motorcycle for $10,000?
414. No. He bought it for 8,000.
415. What did Tim do with the spare $2,000?
416. He purchased new tires for 300 or $400.
     Acceptable: 300 or 400 dollars
417. Tim also repaid his mom $200.00. I believe the exact amount was $192.75.
418. Our company's headquarters are at 246 Park Avenue, Suite 600, Dallas, Texas 75201.
419. Her childhood home was at 567 Elm Street, Denver.
420. For every returned check, there is a $29.95 fee.
421. Did you see the soup on sale for 99 cents each?
422. Yes. That's a savings of about $1.50 each.
423. Buy a dozen and save $18.
424. The conference will take place at 333 Convention Center Boulevard, Las Vegas, Nevada 89109.
425. The office is located at One 13th Street, Suite 405, Chicago, Illinois 60601.
     Not: 1 13th Street

53

Numbers: Formatting an Ordinal, Percentage, or Fraction

426. I bought 8 acres of my parents' property or 10 percent of what they own.
427. Was Ron eight years old at the time? [no correction]
     <u>Or</u> (if technically significant): 8 years old
428. My height is 5 feet 8 inches.
429. The new law needs a two-thirds majority to pass.
430. The report showed five-eighths of students need financial aid.
431. The cut was 3/32 of an inch deep.
432. I failed the quiz. I only got 4/10 of the questions correct.
433. The second step in the chemistry experiment is to add 0.3 ounces of water.
434. I placed ninth in the speed competition. [no correction]
435. Did Morgan place 10th or 11th in the speed competition?
     <u>Not</u>: tenth or 11th
436. The room is 10 feet by 15 feet: 150 square feet.
437. The new 4 percent fee and 8 percent tax compounds to a 12.3 percent increase.
438. Is your 10-year-old son in the fourth or fifth grade?
     <u>Acceptable</u>: 4th or 5th grade [no correction]
439. I just measured the grain silo level and it is 4/5 full.
440. Babe Ruth's batting average was .342.
     <u>Not</u>: 0.342

Numbers: Miscellaneous Number Formatting

441. My height is 6 feet 2 inches; my brother is six, three.
442. Thirteen times 13 is 169.
443. The policy in question is Section 4, paragraph 12.
444. A detailed timeline of the incident can be found on pages 285–291.
     <u>Or</u>: pages 285 to 291
445. My phone number is 777-111-2222.
446. My social security number is 333-00-1111.
447. For Question No. 49, $300 was stolen, not $250.
448. The recipe called for an 8-to-6 ratio of oranges to lemons.
449. I am quoting from page 103, line 9.
450. There were 30-odd students in the classroom when the fire alarm went off.
     <u>Acceptable</u>: thirty-odd students
451. The scientific discoveries of the seventeenth century laid the foundation for modern science.

452. Please refer to Article XI, Section 3, for clarification.
453. Sarah spent 10-some-odd minutes looking for her misplaced keys.
    Acceptable: ten-some-odd minutes
454. The manufacturing process is described on page 23, Figure 2.
455. During 2020–2022, the economic effects of the U.S. pandemic totaled an estimated $4 trillion.
    Or: During 2020 to 2022
456. Is your work telephone number 333-456-9999, Extension 123?
457. Is your social security number really 777-77-7777?
458. World War II occurred during the 1940s.
459. We need to review Chapter VIII for the exam.
460. The novel was 150-something pages long.

Abbreviation
461. The U.S. national debt per taxpayer is $260,000.
462. The Greek Battle of Marathon occurred in 490 BC.
    Acceptable (Gregg): B.C.
463. Is it true, Dr. Cooper, that you failed to perform a complete examination?
464. How many local CEOs attended the city budget meeting?
465. Dr. Bell, DDS, has been my dentist for 20 years.
466. The report states, "approximate vehicle speed: 45 mph."
467. Ms. Anderson, CEO, married Mr. Smith Sr., Ph.D.
468. How many TVs do you have in your home, Mr. Jones?
469. Okay. Did you steal the money, jewelry, et cetera?
470. I told the 911 operator to come ASAP.
471. The CIA's case files are under tight security.
472. Did you hear about Dr. J. and her groundbreaking research in medicine?
473. The Defendant has five known aka's.
474. NASA's recent discovery generated excitement in the scientific community.
475. Mr. X will be the CEO of the company.

476. Logan suddenly left his job because (1) poor pay, (2) poor management, and (3) long commute.

Or (not preferred): Logan suddenly left his job because, one, poor pay; two, poor management; and, three, long commute.

477. I left my trash cans out too long and got a $50 fine from the City of New York.

478. Isabella passed the final speed test. She and her boyfriend went out to dinner.

Or: speed test; she and

479. I saw the car in the corner of my eye at the last second. Unfortunately, I was unable to avoid the collision.

Or: last second; unfortunately, I was

480. Did Liam ask, "What shall we do tonight for dinner?"

481. The Defendant was ID'd in the police **lineup** by Emma.

482. The crack in the windshield measured 7/16 of an inch across.

483. According to our records, the date of loss is September 5, 2018.

484. The detained teens included a 13-, 15-, and 17-year-old.

485. I cannot believe Jackson likes cooked carrots, and if you can believe this, he also likes other vegetables.

Acceptable: cooked carrots; and if

486. Sophia was tardy—wasn't she to the best of your knowledge—to work each day?

487. Punctuation mastery is a **lifelong** journey.

488. My mother called my about the situation: the water heater stopped working, and there is no hot water.

Acceptable: situation: The

Or: situation. The

Or: situation; the

489. Did Mr. Pearson file a claim in Lake County Superior Court?

490. Did you sell the classic '57 Chevy at the car auction in May 2017?

491. I took aspirin for my headache. Isn't Tylenol better?

492. The probation officer reported that he contacted a male and female living at the recently added address in the old case **file; that** the couple stated they are renters who had moved into the home in either June or July of **2018; and that** James had not stopped by to see them or been seen in the area for a long time.

 Or: file, that . . . 2018, and that

493. The poorly constructed deck cost me $5,000 to remove and rebuild.

494. I bought several tomato sauce cans for $0.60 each and saved $2.

495. Riley Walker, lieutenant in the Salvation Army, helped organize the winter clothing drive.

496. Amy responded, "I know my rights and plan to exercise them."

497. To my daughter's Catholic baptism, I invited Zoe, my spiritual advisor; Silas, my accountant for ten years; and Rose, my closest friend.

498. The Sun City Pedestrian Committee has a no-nonsense attitude even on **lighthearted** matters.

499. My lawyer's advice is to take the 15-year deal.

500. Wyatt minds his *p*'s and *q*'s well for a third-grade student.

General Practice 2:

501. The question is this: How was your **weeklong** trip to Hawaii?

502. Well, I own, truth be told, 12 dogs and 3 cats.

503. Did you add 0.8 ounces of vanilla extract? Did it taste as you hoped?

504. The flight took off at four o'clock in the morning, and it landed at 7:15 a.m.

 Acceptable: 4 o'clock

505. Mia passed the **midterm**, didn't she?

506. The question is, Why not attend the conference?

507. I mailed the check. However, I forgot to sign it.

 Or: check; however, I

508. Did Ms. Robinson, president of PharmCo, announced the stock split?

509. Speak louder, please.

510. While in the Big Apple, I stayed in a small, quaint hotel near Times Square.

511. THE COURT: We will recess for lunch until 1:00 p.m.

57

Acceptable: 1 p.m.

512. "The exam results won't be available until Friday," Alex remarked.

513. Lucas wrote Sophia a love poem; hence he loves her.
    Or: poem. Hence he

514. Ashley, my **roommate**, forgot to set the alarm clock for 5:45.

515. Please give the 100-page document to the bailiff, Mr. Williams.

516. The estimated cost to repair the bridge is between $800,000 and $1,200,000.

517. I booked the meeting room for 1:30 p.m., and if you cancel for any reason, there will be a $200 fee.
    Acceptable: 1:30 p.m., and if

518. We selected a cute, cuddly puppy from the shelter.

519. Twenty-seven of every 20 million factory-produced toys are defective.

520. Cora lived with her sister—didn't she per your prior testimony—before she met and moved in with Rebecca?

521. No, I failed to pay the rent by 5:00.
    Acceptable: five [no time correction]

522. Every court reporting student needs practice time, perseverance, et cetera to reach the goal of writing 225 words per minute.
    Gregg: et cetera, to reach

523. I like practicing. To be completely honest, I love capturing the spoken word.
    Or: practicing; to be

524. Objection. Vague and leading.

525. Hannah loaned you $20 last Saturday, correct?

526. I did not want to be home alone, but everyone I called didn't answer.

527. Ethan dropped his wallet **somewhere**. Have you seen it?

528. State and spell your full name, Mr. Bell, for the record, please.

529. After dinner last night with Ms. Cook, Margaret said, "I plan to move to Houston this summer."

530. "I plan to move to Houston," said Ms. Cook after dinner. "I have worked with my current employer since November 2020."

531. I worked **full-time** for five days to **re-form** the damaged statue.

58

532. Attorneys for the Plaintiff and the Defendant stepped outside to argue off the record, not on the record.

533. I packed a lunch for our day hike: peanut butter sandwiches, chips, and bottled water.

534. Mason and Ava married on January 16, 2018, in Seattle, Washington. Do you recall that day?

535. They gave us verbal approval to purchase the new tires. Unfortunately, the amount exceeded their credit limit.
    Or: tires; unfortunately, the

536. The museum opens, doesn't it, at 10:00 a.m. on Tuesdays?
    Acceptable: at 10 a.m. on

537. Did you include the December, January, and February business purchases in the expense report?

538. Yes, I included those months in the decision-making report.

539. No. All the broad-based data was not available at the time.

540. Alice mentioned that she was at work yesterday, but **everyone** I asked didn't see her.

541. While punctuating transcripts, I had a **lightbulb** moment not to **dillydally**.

542. Women's clothing is more expensive than men's clothing. Why is that?

543. Okay. After you received the call, your ETA was 5 minutes, right?

544. My next available appointment times are Monday, 1:30 p.m.; Tuesday, 11:30 a.m.; and Wednesday, 3:00 p.m.

545. Peanut butter sandwiches, chips, and bottled water—I packed a lunch for our day hike.

546. There is a mistake in Figure No. 4, page 37.

547. I mailed the package on Monday. In fact, I mailed it around 12:15 during my lunch break.
    Or: on Monday; in fact, I

548. My last name is spelled S-a-k-s, double i.

549. Because the discrepancy is over $10,000, it is prioritized and called "high risk."

550. Is Labor Day in May or September? I always mix-up that holiday with Memorial Day.

General Practice 3:

551. Margaret, you can never practice too much, right?

552. I cannot make the appointment. I have a hearing in superior court.
    Or: the appointment; I have
553. All right. I must clear this with the president's secretary.
554. I went to the store and bought milk, eggs, bread.
555. I recently bought 12 Apple computers for my business, and I own 1 Apple computer at home too.
556. I have been to the Eiffel Tower, and while I was in France, I took over 150 photographs.
    Acceptable: Tower; and while
557. Is it true that Dr. Cooper, of Lower Michigan WeCare Health Care Group, examined you in July 2021?
558. I remember July 4, 2016, as a cool **summer's** day.
559. Nora witnessed the armed robbery. Her husband missed it because he ran into a college friend.
    Or: armed robbery; her husband
560. We were enjoying the movie when someone yelled: "Fire. Get out."
561. Did you catch the Dallas Cowboys game last night?
562. I watch what people call "nerd TV": shows on comic books and superheroes.
563. Admit it. You returned to the scene of the crime, didn't you?
564. Seventy-five gallons of diesel fuel spilled on the roadway after the truck lost control and hit a tree.
565. You speak super fast. Are you from the East Coast?
566. *Zubov v. Williams* is a 1954 Greene County, Illinois, patent infringement case.
567. Billy has had only one good friend since childhood: Lydia.
568. The approved budget for Jackson County totals $214 million.
569. Anna, upon secretly paying the maître d', was immediately seated in the busy restaurant.
570. Who yelled, quote/unquote, "Fire," in the packed restaurant?
571. I believe it was Mark, a 40-year-old man with a tattoo that covers about fifty percent of his arm.
    Note: The age likely has a technical significance while the tattoo amount does not.
572. Melissa knew it was better to pay $20 for 12 candles, rather than $2 each.
573. My boss harps on the dos and don'ts.

574. Only three witnesses—a bartender, a toxicologist, and a bar patron—were called as witnesses by the **defendant's** attorney.
575. Molly got on the old-fashioned bus, didn't she, for the **downtown** city tour?
576. She refused to agree to the contract terms unless Adam did one thing: apologize for his short-sighted behavior.
577. Did Caleb take the wrong coat by mistake, or did he take it without asking? Do you know?
578. I tracked my package online as it went through Nashville, Tennessee; Saint Louis, Missouri; and Wichita, Kansas.
     Acceptable: St. Louis
579. Tom, how many s's are in dessert?
580. Did your wife have the youngest daughter at home: 2398 Fifth Avenue, Milwaukee, Wisconsin.
581. No. Our daughter was born at the hospital, and the attending physician was Dr. Albert Torre.
582. Unfortunately, the two-hour tennis match was not an action-packed event.
583. Broken glass, twisted metal, and dripping radiator fluid— debris littered the fresh crash site.
584. A woman rushed to a heavily damaged car and asked the driver, "Are you okay?"
585. The driver moaned, "You're an angel, aren't you?"
586. Scott dreamed of only thing for three consecutive nights: The delivery person would finally arrive with his new Stenograph steno machine.
     Or: consecutive nights. The delivery
     Or: consecutive nights; the delivery
587. When I started the car, the stereo volume was on maximum; but James, my son who last drove the car, denies "crankin' it up."
588. The stereo speaker, however, was damaged and needed to be repaired. Unfortunately, my son didn't have the money to fix it.
     Or: be repaired; unfortunately, my
589. As a result, my son got a part-time, decent-earning job to pay the repair bill of $349.95.
590. Keith, my son, needed to work only two months; and he paid the repair bill.
591. Sadie and Ava went ice skating together, yet neither of them knew how to ice skate.

592. Their friends debated if ice skating was a worst-case or best-case situation for them.
593. Upon arriving at the ice rink, they took a free **beginners'** class.
594. The beginners' class was divided into no-, little-, and some-experience groups.
595. Paul Stone Jr., PhD, founded the hi-tech firm in 1986.
596. I can arrange a meeting with Mr. Stone this afternoon, but if you are not available, I can see if Mr. Stone can meet tomorrow at 8:00 a.m.
    Acceptable: this afternoon; but if
    Acceptable: 8 a.m.
597. Mr. Stone is not available tomorrow, Friday, at nine o'clock, correct?
    Acceptable: 9 o'clock
598. No. Mr. Stone is a nice, friendly guy, and his schedule is generally full.
599. Has Evan read the recent article "Free Time" in the *New York Times?* It's in Section D, page 5.
600. Yes, she it. You should read *Twenty-Five Hours a Day*, a book the author wrote in 2019.

Made in United States
Troutdale, OR
12/13/2024

26395933R00040